A Benjamin Blog
and his Inquisitive Dog
Guide

Germany

Anita Ganeri

a Capstone company — publishers for children

Raintree is an imprint of Capstone Global Library Limited, a company incorporated in England and Wales having its registered office at 7 Pilgrim Street, London, EC4V 6LB – Registered company number: 6695582

www.raintree.co.uk
myorders@raintree.co.uk

Edited by Helen Cox Cannons
Designed by Philippa Jenkins and Tim Bond
Original illustrations © Capstone Global Library Limited 2015
Original map illustration by Oxford Designers and Illustrators
Ben and Barko Illustrated by Sernur ISIK
Picture research by Svetlana Zhurkin
Production by Helen McCreath
Originated by Capstone Global Library Limited
Printed and bound in China

ISBN 978 1 406 29834 5
19 18 17 16 15
10 9 8 7 6 5 4 3 2 1

British Library Cataloguing in Publication Data
A full catalogue record for this book is available from the British Library.

Acknowledgements
We would like to thank the following for permission to reproduce photographs: Alamy: Bildarchiv Monheim GmbH, 6; Dreamstime: Kuan Leong Yong, 7, Victormro, cover; Getty Images: Ulrich Baumgarten, 15; iStockphoto: rotofrank, 25, totalpics, 17; Newscom: ABACA/DPA/Jan Woitas, 24, picture alliance/Arco Images/G. Schulz, 11, picture alliance/Chromorange/Alexander Bernhard, 16, Zuma Press/Hemis/John Frumm, 23; Shutterstock: Brent Hofacker, 20, canadastock, 4, chbaum, 9, FamVeld, 14, flowgraph, 28, Jenny Sturm, 27, ksl, 13, Laszlo Szirtesi, 22, Luciano Morpurgo, 10, Marcel Wenk, 8, Noppasin, 12, Olaf Schulz, 19, Roberto Zocchi, 26, 29, Scirocco340, 18, YaiSirichai, 21.

Some words are shown in bold, **like this**. You can find out what they mean by looking in the glossary.

Contents

Welcome to Germany!

Hello! My name's Benjamin Blog and this is Barko Polo, my **inquisitive** dog. (He's named after ancient ace explorer **Marco Polo**.) We have just got back from our latest adventure – exploring Germany. We put this book together from some of the blog posts we wrote on the way.

Country borders

DENMARK

Baltic Sea

•Kiel

North Sea

•Hamburg

Elbe

THE
NETHERLANDS

•Bremen

POLAND

Berlin ■

Balver Höhle
•

G E R M A N Y

•Düsseldorf
•Cologne

BELGIUM

Rhine

Frankfurt
•

Main

LUXEMBOURG

CZECH
REPUBLIC

FRANCE

N

Danube

•Munich

Lake Constance

▲ Zugspitze

SWITZERLAND

AUSTRIA

BARKO'S BLOG-TASTIC GERMANY FACTS

Germany is a large country in Europe. On land, it
has borders with nine other countries – Denmark,
the Netherlands, Belgium, Luxembourg, France,
Switzerland, Austria, the Czech Republic and Poland.

The story of Germany

We're starting our tour in Aachen, in the west of Germany. This was the capital city of **Emperor** Charlemagne (AD 747–814), one of the most important leaders in German history. He is buried in this magnificent gold-and-silver **casket** in Aachen Cathedral.

BARKO'S BLOG-TASTIC GERMANY FACTS

After World War II, Germany was split into two countries – West Germany and East Germany. The city of Berlin was also divided by a high concrete wall. In 1989, the Berlin Wall was pulled down, and Germany became one country again.

Mountains, forests and rivers

Posted by: Ben Blog | 19 June at 12 noon

Next, we headed south to the Zugspitze in Bavaria, on the border between Germany and Austria. At 2,962 metres (9,718 feet), it is the highest mountain in Germany. Instead of climbing, we're taking the cable car up. I'm hoping to get a snap of the cross on the top.

BARKO'S BLOG-TASTIC GERMANY FACTS

The beautiful Black Forest in south-west Germany gets its name from its dark, **coniferous** trees. It is a brilliant place to go hiking – the longest trail is around 280 kilometres (174 miles) long.

We're taking a boat trip along the River Rhine, which flows from Switzerland through Germany. I wanted to see the famous Lorelei rock. Legend says that it is home to a beautiful **maiden** with golden hair. You can hear her singing, if you listen carefully.

BARKO'S BLOG-TASTIC GERMANY FACTS
The Wadden Sea National Park is a huge stretch of marshes and **mudflats** along the German coast of the North Sea. It's a brilliant spot for birdwatching – look at that Arctic tern!

Super cities

Welcome to Berlin, the capital city of Germany. It is famous for the Reichstag (**parliament** building), Tierpark (zoo) and Fernsehturm (television tower). This is the Brandenburg Gate. For years, no one was allowed through the gate until the Berlin Wall fell in 1989.

BARKO'S BLOG-TASTIC GERMANY FACTS

Hamburg is the city with the second-biggest population in Germany. It lies on the River Elbe and is also the country's main **port**. Every year, in May, there is a party for the port's birthday!

Guten Morgen!

I've been trying to learn some German while we're here. *Guten Morgen* means "Good morning". *Auf Wiedersehen* means "Goodbye". If you know someone very well, you can say *Tschüss!* for goodbye instead. *Ich heisse Benjamin Blog* means "My name is Benjamin Blog".

14

BARKO'S BLOG-TASTIC GERMANY FACTS

Nearly 81 million people live in Germany. Most of them are Germans. There are also many people from countries such as Turkey and Italy who moved to Germany to find work.

German children start school when they are six years old. Their first day at school is marked by a special gift called a *Schultüte* (school bag). This is a big paper cone, decorated with pictures and stickers, and filled with toys, sweets, pens, pencils and books.

BARKO'S BLOG-TASTIC GERMANY FACTS

Just under three-quarters of German people live in cities. City people live in blocks of flats or apartments. This apartment block is built in the Altbau style, which means "Old Building".

It was time to do some Christmas shopping, so we headed to the brilliant Christmas market in Nuremberg. There are 180 stalls there, decorated in red-and-white cloth. There are lots of yummy things to eat, including plum people and gingerbread men.

BARKO'S BLOG-TASTIC GERMANY FACTS

Many German people are Christians, and there are beautiful churches all over Germany. This is the magnificent Cologne Cathedral. Its spires are more than 157 metres (515 feet) tall.

Feeling hungry

Germany is famous for making *wurst* (that's German for sausage). There are over 150 kinds of *wurst*. I was hungry and decided to try some *bratwurst*. You can eat it in a bread roll, or with *sauerkraut* (pickled cabbage), potato salad or a dollop of mustard. Yum!

BARKO'S BLOG-TASTIC GERMANY FACTS

Schwarzwälder Kirschtorte (Black Forest gateau) is a delicious German cake. It is made from layers of chocolate cake, with whipped cream and cherries in between.

Sport and music

Posted by: Ben Blog | 1 February at 3.32 p.m.

Our next stop was the Allianz Arena in Munich. Barko and I are here to watch a football match. This is the home ground of Bayern Munich, one of the top teams in Germany. German people love football. Germany won the World Cup in Brazil in 2014.

BARKO'S BLOG-TASTIC GERMANY FACTS

The Berlin Philharmonic Orchestra is one of the leading orchestras in the world. It plays music by many famous German **composers**, including Beethoven, Bach and Brahms.

From fast cars to wind farms

Posted by: Ben Blog | 17 March at 9.01 a.m.

Car making is one of Germany's main industries, and German factories make some of the world's fastest and best-quality cars. This factory in Leipzig produces around 500 Porsche cars every day. We're off to take a tour of the factory and see how they are made.

BARKO'S BLOG-TASTIC GERMANY FACTS

This huge wind farm in Emden, north-west Germany, is one of the biggest in Europe. **Wind turbines**, like these, turn the power of the wind into electrical power.

And finally...

Our trip is nearly over but we have saved the best until last. Here is a snap that I took of Neuschwanstein Castle in Bavaria. It perches on a mountaintop and was built by King Ludwig II. Sleeping Beauty's castle at Disneyland is based on this fairytale place.

26

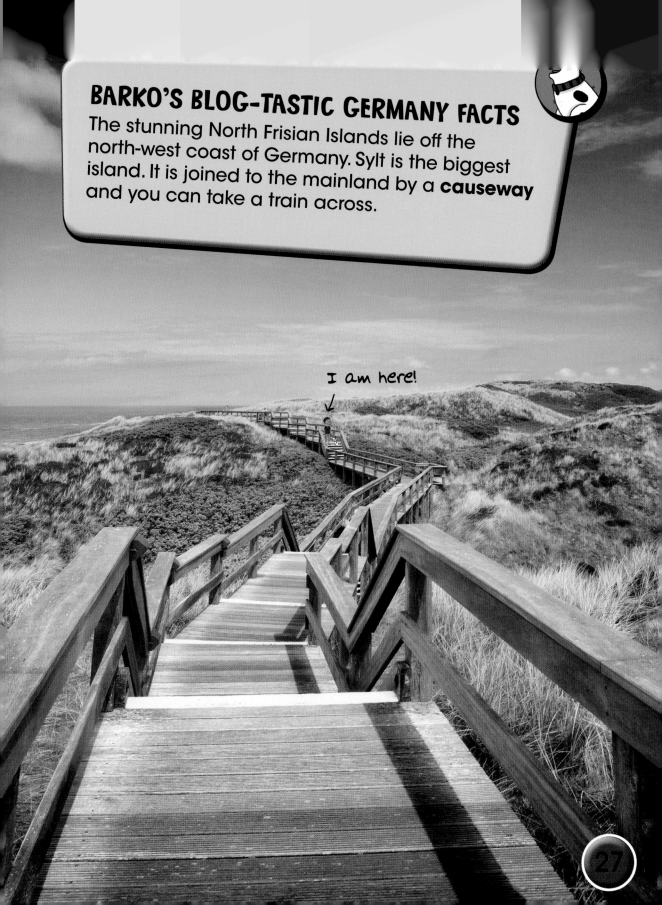

BARKO'S BLOG-TASTIC GERMANY FACTS
The stunning North Frisian Islands lie off the north-west coast of Germany. Sylt is the biggest island. It is joined to the mainland by a **causeway** and you can take a train across.

I am here!

Germany fact file

Area: 357,022 square kilometres
(137,846 square miles)

Population: 80,716,000 (2014)

Capital city: Berlin

Other main cities: Hamburg, Munich, Cologne,
Frankfurt am Main

Language: German

Main religion: Christianity

Highest mountain: Zugspitze (2,962 metres/
9,718 feet)

Longest river: Rhine
(865 kilometres/537 miles long in Germany)

Currency: Euro

Germany quiz

Find out how much you know about Germany with our quick quiz.

1. Which German city was divided in two?
a) Munich
b) Berlin
c) Cologne

2. What does *auf Wiedersehen* mean?
a) Goodbye
b) Good morning
c) How are you?

3. What is *bratwurst*?
a) a type of sausage
b) a type of salad
c) a type of cake

4. Which sport does Bayern Munich play?
a) basketball
b) rugby
c) football

5. What is this?

Answers
1. b
2. a
3. a
4. c
5. Neuschwanstein Castle

Glossary

casket another name for a coffin

causeway raised path or road across water

composer person who writes music

coniferous describes a tree with needles instead of leaves that stays green all year round

emperor ruler of a group of countries, called an empire

inquisitive interested in learning about the world

maiden another name for a girl

Marco Polo explorer who lived from about 1254 to 1324. He travelled from Italy to China.

mudflat flat, muddy land that is covered by sea at high tide

parliament meeting of the rulers of a country

port place where ships are loaded and unloaded

wind turbine machine that turns wind power into electrical power

Find out more

Books

Germany (Countries in Our World), Michael Burgan (Franklin Watts, 2013)

Germany (Countries Around the World), Mary Colson (Raintree, 2012)

Websites

ngkids.co.uk

National Geographic's website has lots of information, photos and maps of countries around the world.

www.worldatlas.com

Packed with information about different countries, this website has flags, time zones, facts and figures, maps and timelines.

Index